YOUR KNOWLEDGE HAS VALUE

AF173329

- We will publish your bachelor's and master's thesis, essays and papers

- Your own eBook and book - sold worldwide in all relevant shops

- Earn money with each sale

Upload your text at www.GRIN.com
and publish for free

Jannika Anne

Transcultural Space as a Multicultural Solution

GRIN Publishing

Bibliographic information published by the German National Library:

The German National Library lists this publication in the National Bibliography; detailed bibliographic data are available on the Internet at http://dnb.dnb.de .

Imprint:

Copyright © 2014 GRIN Verlag GmbH
Print and binding: Books on Demand GmbH, Norderstedt Germany
ISBN: 978-3-656-85980-2

This book at GRIN:

http://www.grin.com/en/e-book/285739/transcultural-space-as-a-multicultural-solution

GRIN - Your knowledge has value

Since its foundation in 1998, GRIN has specialized in publishing academic texts by students, college teachers and other academics as e-book and printed book. The website www.grin.com is an ideal platform for presenting term papers, final papers, scientific essays, dissertations and specialist books.

Visit us on the internet:

http://www.grin.com/

http://www.facebook.com/grincom

http://www.twitter.com/grin_com

TRANSCULTURAL SPACE

RUPRECHT-KARLS-UNIVERSITÄT HEIDELBERG

September 14

Contents

1. Introduction

The times when a politician could rely on references to a stable, homogenized notions of his place and hope to reach his citizens have long been over. Nowadays, the idea of a culture or identity of a place as unchanging, homogenous to the inside and clearly delimited to the outside, has not only been overcome, but also considered as invalid for any moment in time.

Undoubtedly, space is "more than a geographical category, it is also a social concept" (Tamcke et al. 2013, 10) and t is now widely recognized that "where events unfold is integral to how they take shape" (Warf and Arias 2009, 10) Multiculturalism, intercultural projects, tolerance and cooperation have since been the aspiration and slogans of many countries and cities. While a world where people constantly migrate from one place to another makes those discourses highly relevant and necessary, the concepts' limits have also become visible and a need for different approaches becomes evident.

Hence, this paper tries to outline a possible version of transcultural notions of space. The main point is to raise different perspectives and possibly find a solution for conflicts which concepts such as multiculturalism were not able to solve.

First, this paper intends to define transcultural space as it might and would be interpreted in this work. This involves the characteristics, the areas where a transcultural perspective could be particularly useful and the attempt at a working definition. The second section copes with transcultural space in itself, the opportunities it offers, where it might contribute to place-making and urban research and also its limits which have to be mentioned. The third section applies transcultural space perceptions to place, namely Macau. A very short case study investigates if, where and in how far a place can be considered transcultural. The conclusion then summarizes and finalizes the paper.

2. Transcultural Space

2.1. Characteristics, Potential and Possibilities

According to Jonathan Raban, a city can be divided into "soft" and "hard" elements. Raban describes the phenomena as follows:

"The city goes soft; it awaits the imprint of an identity. For better or worse, it invites you to remake it, to consolidate it into a shape you can live in. You, too. Decide who you are, and the city will again assume a fixed form around you. Decide what it is, and your own identity will be revealed" (Raban 1974, 11).

Thus, "places are not given, but produced by human activity" (Prazniak et al. 2001, 15) Transcultural space would be an approach to explain soft place characteristics, interested rather in the social action within and produced by a place, the same actions that cause a continual process of change. This same action is performed by the actors, namely the people living in the place, and only they can create transcultural space and make it meaningful. Consequently, the creators of transcultural spaces are the most significant elements for a transcultural space.

The specificity of place comes from being "constructed out of a particular constellation of social relations, meeting and weaving together at a particular locus, positively integrating the global and the local" (Wyse et al. 2012, 1021). The actors can vary from artists who become instrumental in disseminating art world concepts from abroad (cp. Park 2014, 224) to travellers or immigrants in new places, who develop new negotiation strategies for their integration into the new place (cp. Gazzola in Roncador and Stevens 2002, 281). Transcultural notions agree with Massey's image of place as an event, a "meeting place" (Massey 1994, 154) or Anderson's "contact zones" (Anderson, 1991), without reducing space to that mere functions.

The creation of transcultural spaces is episodic. "It is not that an unwanted repetitive pattern is fixed one time and all is well" (Goering 2013, 139). On the contrary, transcultural space is dynamic and stimulated by the activities of others, causing a constant process of change and evolution.

However, it is also perceptual, created by people from their individual experiences and through their interactions (Wyse et al. 2012, 1035) and scarcely feasible by the "hard elements" of a city. This is the reason why a lasting definition is eventually impossible. Transcultural spaces can be interpreted in many different ways from" the simultaneity of movement, crossings and meaning-making" (Wyse et al. 2012, 1022), "a passage through all particularism and interaction toward a common ground or a common aim" (Tamcke 2013, 147) or in such strategies as the presence of multilingual practices, the portrayal of "in-between," fluid and hybrid characters, and the elaboration of new urban and domestic spaces created through interactions between cultures (Pilar Rodríguez 2013, 177).

Homi Bhabha 'liminal spaces' – fluid and often vague realms of conflict, interactions and mutual assimilation between more powerful and less powerful communities (Bhabha 2004) - have partly been used as a base for transcultural notions of space . Liminal spaces are neither here nor there; they are a collection of transitional qualities 'betwixt and between' states of culture (Turner 1995). For Bhabha, a liminal spaces is a hybrid 'third space' that permits alternative positions to emerge (Bhabha 2004). Perceptions of transcultural spaces remind of this concept although focusing less on assimilation, interaction and seemingly stable power relations. A space can still be transcultural without visible interaction between all the actors and "mutual assimilation" is rather an exception than the rule. Likewise, a transcultural notion of space would attempt to avoid "victimization", the power relation between different groups is believed to be changing according to the situation and it is recognized that allegedly less powerful groups such as migrants have their own defending mechanisms and demand of rights. According to Ma Mung: "Immigrants are now increasingly demanding multiple belonging, not being either from here or over there, but from here and over there. (Ma Mung in Pilar Rodríguez 2013, 180)

2.2. Contribution to Place-Making

Different approaches to urban studies have often reached limits where a transcultural approach might be helpful. Multiculturalism, for instance, does not consider the unequal power relationships between communities in cultures that develops through the unequal and dialectical relations that different cultural groups construct in a given society at a particular point in history (Park 2014, 225). In this section, it will be discussed how a notion of transcultural space can contribute to the current approaches.

Frequently, traditional research situation generated a dividing line between the researcher (as the object) and the researched (the foreign subject) (Kohl 2013, 15). If we believe, as mentioned before, that "material spaces and places are shaped by and reflect the social, ethnic identity and literate practices of those that move through them" (Moje in Wyse et al. 2012, 1021) and transcultural space is meaningful owing to its actors and produced through their action, this 'production' seems to be constituted within 'representation' and a 'narrative' of the self (cp. Hall, 1990). Transcultural space gives more freedom to these stories and with a transcultural lens, it might be possible to create spaces for a more equal communication "if we are willing to put resources at risk and 'create fertile turbulence' through the exchange of personal stories" (Goering 2013, 139). In addition it paves the way to learn from others, extend horizons and search for common ground. This exchange of stories at its best reveals cross-over influences in a place that can result in "novel ways of seeing and being, from whence new identities, cultures and political alignments emerge" (Dear and Flusty 1999, 77).

Furthermore, transcultural space raises more "universal" questions rather than being just a reaction to a specific country, attempting to cope with transcultural space could be a way to understand an 'open global' society that recognises difference. Transcultural space steps away from the idea that place is necessarily something that connects one specific community with a site. People do not want to be caught in a one culture logic (Park 2014, 227). Many people cannot simply define what is home. It can be "here, and there, or in-between and nowhere" (Park 2014, 226). Homogenized notions of place do not fit and transcultural space could provide a site for the freedom to belong to more than one place. Ideally, it opposes the construct of singular traditional cultures, and instead breaks down divisionary boundaries. Rather than a sense of place defined by a close connection between a singular form of identity and place, and a need for a clear sense of boundaries around a place separating it from the world outside, place is a process, defined by the outside and a site of multiple identities and histories (Wyse et al. 2012, 1021). Following this definition place interacts with ideas of movement across geographical zones, grounded in shifting associations between local and other places (Wyse et al. 2012, 1035).

Place-relations are often expressed in binaries of familiar/foreign, local/global and same/other (Wyse et al. 2012, 1020). The underlying assumption of assumed dichotomies such as "them" and "us" does not respond to the existing diversity and complexity of the world, in particular in urban spaces (Kohl 2013, 16). The idea of a transcultural space helps to deconstruct this apparent truth.

Such as every other approach, the idea of transcultural space has its own limits and problems. Frequently, a transcultural space is perceived as term for places of assimilation, where difference is supressed in order to create a global, common culture. In their recently published book "Interkulturalität", Hamid Reza Yousefi and Ina Braun define transculturality as a common culture beyond cultural peculiarities (Tamcke 2013, 147). Notwithstanding, a transcultural space is, on the contrary, explicitly meant to be a site for difference and does not aim at an existence beyond all cultural peculiarities.

3. Applicability: Macau, a "real world" example of transcultural space?

The concluding question for the last section of this paper is what happens when the method is actually applied to a region? Is there something like a transcultural space in "the real world"?

Macau with its fast-changing landscape, the many different worlds in a small place and its colourful history of contacts could be one of those spaces. After the construction boom in the 1980s until the 1990s covering the small territory with concrete towers (Amaro 1998, 232) and Portugal's return of the Macau to the People's Republic of China in 1999, the monopoly of the local gaming industry was withdrawn and, Macau became the world's most lucrative casino gaming site, generating revenues of US $28 billion in 2012 and Macau's resorts attracted 28 million visitors in 2012 (Simpson 2014, 824), adding to the high number of expatriate workers, migrant workers and immigrants. Macau resorts circulate large numbers of locals, expatriate workers and Chinese tourists who together represent a temporary "fictitious population", interacting in moments of 'immaterial' labour and consumption (Simpson 2014, 825). Consequently, Macau is confronted with a huge amount of travellers on a daily basis.

Not only the people, but also money from many different places flows in and out of Macau. The city has been the site of substantial foreign investment, chiefly from transnational concerns from the Australia, the United States, and Hong Kong, which are drawn to Macau because it is the only place in China where gaming is legal. Transnational finance capital invested in Macau takes the shape of themed and narrated casino resorts, which might be considered "fictitious architecture" displaying historical and cultural scenarios of other times and places (Simpson 2014, 825).

Since the 1980s, Macau has become an Eldorado for the Portuguese as it was at the end of the decade XVI. Many Portuguese dream of the Orient, with high salaries, good reforms that are more and more difficult to obtain in Europe (Amaro 1998, 200). For Beijing the city plays a formative role in a new Chinese tourist imaginary. According to Macau-based scholars, Macau might be understood as a *"laboratory of consumption"* where selected Chinese tourists are immersed in an environment that naturalizes and normalizes the urban imaginary (Simpson 2014, 825). In architecture, gastronomy and event, Portuguese and Chinese elements are negotiated just as the countries' political and Macau-related visions and projects. A telling image for Macau is "the old is kept and preserved and the new is built among and around it" (Wong and Feng 2014, xxv).

Apart from the hybrid, post-colonial Macau outside, the casinos create new worlds within buildings. Transnational finance capital invested in Macau today is transformed into narrated casino resorts, which might be interpreted as *"fictitious architecture"* since those structures display historical and cultural motifs of other times and places (Simpson 2014, 825).

In Macau, people belonging to different cultures live together in a few square kilometre, sharing the same economic and political structure (Amaro 1998, 174). The different sides meet in conflict and cooperation, isolation and interaction. Liu Denghan once described Macau as follows: "Superficially, the diversity of cultures in Macau is multicolored like a cocktail that consists of different spirits, the Eastern one and the Western one. Once examined closely, different cultures remain distinct, just like a cocktail with well-defined layers and these layers do not mingle or compound" (Wong and Feng 2014, xix). On other occasions Macau has been accused for being 'globally connected and locally disconnected' (Castells in Simpson 2014, 826). However, particularly among the young generation, there has been a strong movement towards more place-specific, local awareness, more affection for Macau and more interest for its different sides.

With this approach, Macau could be called a transcultural space where the life of most different people collide without having to romanticize it as a "contact zone" or "meeting point between East and West". Sometimes, reterritorialization can result in remediation (Bond and Rapson, 2). Following this, perhaps it can be argued that the Portuguese spatial features were remediated for Macau territory. The challenge is to recognize without judging prematurely that contact between Portugal and China in Macau is far from harmonious and displays accentuated power disparities. Transculturality explores how the occurring misunderstandings and conflicts can be productive (Wyse et al. 2012, 1023).

4. Conclusion

Even though still promoted by politicians and several scholarly approaches, nowadays it seems an oversimplification in a world in motion to encourage assimilation by persuading, for instance, politics of compulsory and urgent need to learn the local language of one country (Pilar Rodríguez 2013, 182). The image of a linguistically, culturally and religious homogenous place has been an illusion of past centuries and is ever less convincing. On the contrary, the current urban situations show realities of places that might have to result not only in alteration of prevailing structures and institutions (Dear and Flusty 1999, 77), but first of all in a new way of thinking about place. Transculturality recognizes that urbanism exists as a form of control over human and nature activities and ecologies (Dear and Flusty 1999, 75). The complex strategies and patterns to be found among urban places and people can certainly not be understood by one universal concept only. This short paper attempted to demonstrate that transcultural space could turn out to be a promising way to look at the fast-changing "soft elements" (Raban 1974) of global cities, namely urban patterns and behaviours, urban people. The aim was to show that it could be an appropriate method to examine urban behaviour since "transcultural existence is not a vision, nothing that politics is supposed to bring about; rather, it is a reality that has always been noticeable in human life" (Tamcke 2013, 148). Transculturality, as interpreted in this work, has potential to deal with the reality of everyday situations in different places and to adopt an inclusive view on a city and its citizens without supressing their individuality.

To conclude, a quote suggesting that transcultural communication is possible if we recognize that it has to be created through communication:

"I am not you, as you are not me. Yet I am not just separated from you, as you are not just separated from me. There is something of you in me, as there is something of me in you. Therefore, when we have to interact, I deal with you in me, as you deal with me in you for a better understanding of each other, as a value in itself." (Goering 2013, 135).

5. References

Amaro, Ana M. 1998. *Das cabanas de palha às torres de betão: Assim cresceu Macau*. 1. ed. Colecção Estudos e documentos. Lisboa: Universidade Técnica de Lisboa, Instituto Superior de Ciências Sociais e Políticas; Livros do Oriente.

Anderson, Benedict R. O'G. 1991. *Imagined communities: Reflections on the origin and spread of nationalism*. Rev. and extended ed. London, New York: Verso.

Bhabha, Homi K. 2004. *The location of culture*. Routledge classics. London, New York: Routledge.

Bond, Lucy, and Jessica Rapson. "Introduction." In *The transcultural turn: Interrogating memory between and beyond borders*, edited by Lucy Bond and Jessica Rapson. Media and cultural memory/ Medien und kulturelle Erinnerung volume 15.

Dear, Michael, and Steven Flusty. 1999. "Cultural Mapping: The Postmodern Urban Condition." In *Spaces of culture: City, nation, world*, edited by Mike Featherstone and Scott Lash, 65–85. Theory, culture & society. London, Thousand Oaks, Calif. Sage.

Goering, Elizabeth. 2013. "Entering the Third Dimension A CMM (Coordinated Management of Meaning) Analysis of Transculturalism in Inter/Action." In Tamcke, Jong, Klein, Waal, Margriet van der, and Altuna-Garccía de Salazar, Asier, *Europe - space for transcultural existence?* 133–42.

Kohl, Philipp. 2013. *Aufwertung und Identität im transkulturellen Raum: Divergierende Rezeptionen zweier Mannheimer Stadtquartiere*. SpringerLink : Bücher. Wiesbaden: Springer VS.

Massey, Doreen B. 1994. *Space, place, and gender*. Minneapolis: University of Minnesota Press.

Park, Jeong-Ae. 2014. "Korean Artists in Transcultural Spaces: Constructing New National Identities." *International Journal of Art & Design Education* 33 (2): 223–34. doi:10.1111/j.1476-8070.2014.01775.x.

Pilar Rodríguez, Maria. 2013. "Multiculturalism versus Transculturality." In Tamcke, Jong, Klein, Waal, Margriet van der, and Altuna-Garccía de Salazar, Asier, *Europe - space for transcultural existence?* 175–84.

Prazniak, Roxann, Arif Dirlik, John B. Childs, Arturo Escobar, Jonathan Friedman, Wendy Harcourt, Peter Kwong et al., eds. 2001. *Places and Politics in an Age of Globalization.* Lanham: Rowman & Littlefield Publishers. http://gbv.eblib.com/patron/FullRecord.aspx?p=1385112.

Raban, Jonathan. 1974. *Soft City.* New York: E.P. Dutton.

Roncador, Sônia, and Cristina Stevens. 2002. "Quando o tio Sam pegar no tamborim: Uma perspectiva transcultural do Brasil." *Revista de Crítica Literaria Latinoamericana* 28 (55): 280–82. doi:10.2307/4531217.

Simpson, Tim. 2014. "Macau Metropolis and Mental Life: Interior Urbanism and the Chinese Imaginary." *Int J Urban Reg Res* 38 (3): 823–42. doi:10.1111/1468-2427.12139.

Tamcke, Martin, Janny d. Jong, Lars Klein, Waal, Margriet van der, and Altuna-Garccía de Salazar, Asier, eds. 2013. *Europe - space for transcultural existence?* Studies in Euroculture 1. Göttingen: Universitätsverlag Göttingen.

Tamcke, Martin. 2013. "Introduction: On the Path to Transculturality?" In Tamcke, Jong, Klein, Waal, Margriet van der, and Altuna-Garccía de Salazar, Asier, *Europe - space for transcultural existence?* 143–49.

Turner, Victor W. 1995. *The ritual process: Structure and anti-structure.* The Lewis Henry Morgan lectures 1966. New York: Aldine de Gruyter.

Warf, Barney, and Santa Arias. 2009. *The spatial turn: Interdisciplinary perspectives.* Routledge studies in human geography 26. London, New York: Routledge.

Wong, Katrine K., and Feng. 2014. "Introduction." In *Macao - cultural interaction and literary representations*, edited by Katrine K. Wong, Wei, C. X. George, and Zhiliang Wu. Routledge studies in the modern history of Asia 86.

Wyse, Dominic, Maria Nikolajeva, Emma Charlton, Gabrielle C. Hodges, Pam Pointon, and Liz Taylor. 2012. "Place-related identity, texts, and transcultural meanings." *British Educational Research Journal* 38 (6): 1019–39. doi:10.1080/01411926.2011.608251.